The Return Of The

LONE IGUANA

P9-CNH-922

Other FoxTrot Books by Bill Amend

FoxTrot
Pass the Loot
Black Bart Says Draw
Eight Yards, Down and Out
Bury My Heart at Fun-Fun Mountain
Say Hello to Cactus Flats
May The Force Be With Us, Please
Take Us To Your Mall
At Least This Place Sells T-Shirts
Come Closer, Roger, There's a Mosquito on Your Nose
Welcome to Jasorassic Park

Anthologies

FoxTrot: The Works
FoxTrot *en masse*
Enormously FoxTrot
Wildly FoxTrot
FoxTrot Beyond a Doubt
Camp FoxTrot

THE RETURN OF THE
LONE
IGUANA

A FoxTrot Collection by Bill Amend

Andrews and McMeel
A Universal Press Syndicate Company
Kansas City

FoxTrot is distributed internationally by Universal Press Syndicate.

The Return of the Lone Iguana copyright © 1996 by Bill Amend. All rights reserved. Printed in the United States of America. No part of this book may be used or reproduced in any manner whatsoever without written permission except in the case of reprints in the context of reviews. For information, write Andrews and McMeel, a Universal Press Syndicate Company, 4900 Main Street, Kansas City, Missouri 64112.

ISBN: 0-8362-1027-1

Library of Congress Catalog Card Number: 95-81037

Printed on recycled paper.

02 BAM 10 9 8 7 6 5

─────────── ATTENTION: SCHOOLS AND BUSINESSES ───────────

Andrews and McMeel books are available at quantity discounts with bulk purchase for educational, business, or sales promotional use. For information, please write to: Special Sales Department, Andrews and McMeel, 4900 Main Street, Kansas City, Missouri 64112.

HOWDY, MA'AM.

JASON, WHAT ARE YOU DOING?!

WELL, WORD IS THINGS ARE GETTIN' A MITE UGLY 'ROUND THESE PARTS AND THE WAY I SEE IT, THERE'S ONLY ONE THING THAT CAN SET THINGS RIGHT.

WHAT'S THAT?

(TA'DA) THE RETURN OF THE LONE IGUANA!

DIDN'T WE GO THROUGH THIS LAST SUMMER?

OK, THE RETURN OF THE RETURN OF THE LONE IGUANA.

YOU KNOW, IN CASE YOU THINK I ENJOY PEELING YOUR SISTER OFF THE CEILING...

WHAT'S GOING ON?!

WHY IS THE WILLIAM TELL OVERTURE PLAYING ON THE STEREO AT SEVEN O'CLOCK IN THE MORNING?!

THIS CAN'T BE HAPPENING! IT'S LIKE A BAD DREAM!

THE LONE IGUANA SAYS DON'T TOUCH THAT DIAL.

... ONLY WEIRDER.

PARDON ME, MISSY, BUT HAVE YOU SEEN THIS VARMINT?

SHE'S WANTED FOR ILLEGALLY IMPERSONATING A HORSE.

'COURSE SHE GOT THE FACE AND BUTT ALL MIXED UP.

... THAT AND ATTEMPTED MURDER.

JASON, GO AWAY.

5

THIRTY MORE MINUTES...

TEN MORE MINUTES...

TWO MORE... ONE MORE... YEEHA! QUITTIN' TIME!

THIRTEEN MORE HOURS...

I HAD MORE, BUT PAIGE MADE ME EAT THEM.

JASON, GO AWAY!

JASON, GO AWAY!

JASON, GO AWAY!

I CAN SEE WHERE THE "LONE" LABEL COMES FROM.

WHAT HAPPENED TO THE LONE IGUANA?

HE RODE OFF INTO THE SUNSET.

FINALLY.

ALL HE LEFT BEHIND WAS THIS SILVER SUCTION DART.

JASON, I CAN'T BELIEVE YOU'D GO TO ALL THE TROUBLE OF PAINTING ONE OF THESE.

THEN AGAIN...

I GUESS HE KNEW WERE-IGUANAS WERE AFOOT.

FoxTrot
BILL AMEND

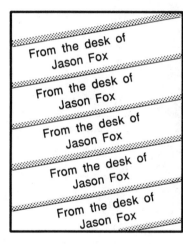

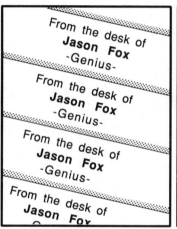

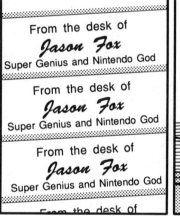

FoxTrot
BILL AMEND

OH, MAN, I HAD THE WORST DREAM LAST NIGHT.

SCHOOL STARTED TWO WEEKS EARLY AND THEY CHANGED MY SCHEDULE SO I HAD NOTHING BUT MATH CLASSES.

WITH QUIZZES EVERY DAY.

ICK. I'M SO GLAD I WOKE UP.

NO DOUBT.

OH, MAN, I HAD THE BEST DREAM LAST NIGHT.

JASON FOX, YOU'VE SPENT PRACTICALLY YOUR WHOLE SUMMER COOPED UP IN FRONT OF THAT COMPUTER!

ENOUGH ALREADY! I WANT YOU BOYS TO PLAY OUTSIDE AND GET SOME FRESH AIR IN THOSE LUNGS FOR A CHANGE! LET'S GO!

AND DON'T COME BACK UNTIL DINNERTIME!

THREE WORDS: HALLELUJAH FOR LAPTOPS.

I'VE GOT YOUR SPARE BATTERY CHARGING UP IN THE GARAGE.

WHERE'S PAIGE?

SHE WENT OUT TO BUY BINDER PAPER.

WHAT? I TOLD HER WE'D DO ALL HER BACK-TO-SCHOOL SHOPPING **NEXT** WEEK!

I TOLD HER TO MAKE A LIST AND—

I THINK SHE NEEDED THE PAPER **FOR** HER LIST.

BUT I'VE GOT PLENTY OF PAPER...

DEFINE "PLENTY."

WHY IS PAIGE DRAGGING A BIG BOX UP THE DRIVEWAY?

QUINCY, SHAKE.

LIE DOWN. ROLL OVER. HEEL. PLAY DEAD. JUMP.

YOU ARE SO PATHETIC.

I SUPPOSE "ATTACK" IS OUT OF THE QUESTION.

WHAT MOVIE DID YOU GET?

"RETURN TO THE PLANET OF THE MAGGOTS."

EEW! GROSS! SICK!

I CAN'T BELIEVE YOU WOULD RENT THIS! I CAN'T BELIEVE YOU WOULD ACTUALLY PAY MONEY TO PUT SOMETHING THIS DISGUSTING ON OUR TV! I CAN'T BELIEVE A MOVIE LIKE THIS EVEN EXISTS!

SO, DID IT JUST START?

I'LL REWIND IT. THE OPENING'S PRETTY IMPORTANT.

HOW DO FOOTBALL PLAYERS REMEMBER ALL THESE PLAYS?

HOW DO FOOTBALL PLAYERS REMEMBER THEIR NAMES?

FoxTrot
BILL AMEND

ATTENTION, WORLD.

I SAID...

HEAR ME, MORTALS. FOR I SPEAK.

YEA, IT IS THE DAWNING OF A NEW AGE.! AN AGE OF OBEDIENCE, OF SERVITUDE, OF DISCIPLINE.!

I HAVE COME FROM ON HIGH TO DELIVER THESE COMMANDMENTS!

...AND DEFY THEM NOT...

FOR THOSE WHO WOULD SHALL SURELY MEET MY FURY!

FOR I AM THE SUPREME AND ALL-POWERFUL NEW GOD OF YOUR WORLD! WA HA HA HA HA.!

NOW, LISTEN WELL. ALL OF YE.

JASON, I WANT YOU TO CLEAN MY ROOM... PAIGE, I WANT YOU TO BAKE ME THOSE COOKIES I LIKE...

I HATE IT WHEN MOM AND DAD LEAVE PETER IN CHARGE.

WHO DOES HE THINK HE IS?!

AMEND

I CAN'T WAIT FOR SCHOOL TO START...

I REALLY CAN'T WAIT FOR SCHOOL TO START...

I REALLY, REALLY, **REEEALLY** CAN'T WAIT FOR SCHOOL TO START...

PETER, THIS IS SO UNLIKE YOU!

READY FOR BACK-TO-SCHOOL SHOPPING, ROUND XII?

PAIGE, CAN'T WE TAKE **ONE** DAY OFF?? AH...

I REMEMBER WHEN I WAS 14, I COULDN'T **WAIT** TILL I WAS OLD ENOUGH TO DRIVE.

WHEN I WAS 15, I WAS PRACTICALLY GOING OUT OF MY **MIND** WITH ANTICIPATION.

AND NOW THAT I FINALLY **AM** 16...

PETER, QUIT YAPPING AND STEP ON IT. THE MALL OPENS IN TWO MINUTES.

...I CAN'T WAIT TILL **YOU** ARE OLD ENOUGH TO DRIVE.

WELL, PETER, YOU'RE ONE LUCKY BROTHER.

OH?

MY SHOPPING LIST IS TWICE AS LONG AS USUAL, MOM IS LETTING ME USE ONE OF HER CREDIT CARDS AND I PACKED US A COUPLE OF ENERGY BARS SO WE CAN SHOP RIGHT THROUGH LUNCHTIME.

IN OTHER WORDS, YOU'RE GOING TO BE IN THIS MALL **ALL DAY LONG**!!!

OH, WAIT — WE HAVE DIFFERING VIEWS ON "LUCK"...

SOMEONE JUST SHOOT ME, PLEASE.

LET'S SEE... IF I GET THIS BLACK BELT, I CAN'T WEAR THE TAN SHOES AND THE BROWN PURSE GOES OUT THE WINDOW.

BUT... IF I DON'T GET THE TAN SHOES, I COULD GET THOSE CUTE RED PANTS THAT WOULD LOOK GREAT WITH THIS BELT **AND** WHICH HAD THAT HOT MATCHING SWEATER-VEST...

IF I **DO** GO WITH THE RED PANTS, HOWEVER, I'D HAVE TO START ALL OVER IN THE EARRING DEPARTMENT BECAUSE THOSE BLUE ONES WOULDN'T MATCH. HMM...

IT'S A LOT LIKE CHESS.

SO WHY DOES IT FEEL LIKE HANGMAN?

WHEW. I'M BEAT.

I SWEAR, WE MUST'VE WALKED UP AND DOWN THIS MALL 20 TIMES TODAY AT LEAST. THINK HOW MANY **MILES** THAT IS!

MY FEET ARE KILLING ME... MY BACK IS KILLING ME... MY LEGS ARE JUST PLAIN POOPED...

THANK HEAVENS WE'RE DOWN TO THE LAST PAGE OF MY SHOPPING LIST.

WILL THERE BE ANY STORES THAT SELL ASPIRIN?

I CAN'T BELIEVE I'VE ACTUALLY FINISHED ALL OF MY BACK-TO-SCHOOL SHOPPING!

I'VE GOT THE PERFECT BACK-TO-SCHOOL OUTFIT... THE PERFECT BACK-TO-SCHOOL PURSE. AN ADORABLE BACK-TO-SCHOOL HAIR-CARE ENSEMBLE... EVERY-THING!

I, PAIGE FOX, AM NOW **READY** FOR SCHOOL TO START!

WHAT ABOUT GETTING NOTEBOOKS AND STUFF?

OOPS.

IF YOU THINK FOR ONE SECOND THAT WE'RE DRIVING BACK TO THAT MALL...

15

FoxTrot
BILL AMEND

This is your brain →

This is your brain on drugs →

This is my sister's brain → ˋ

YOU ALREADY FORGOT YOUR LOCKER COMBINATION?!

MY MEMORY IS REALLY BAD, OK?

PAIGE, WHY DIDN'T YOU WRITE IT ON YOUR HAND OR SOMETHING, THEN?

I WISH I **HAD**.

OH, WAIT— I DID—

YOU WEREN'T KIDDING ABOUT YOUR MEMORY.

SHOOT—NOW WHICH ONE WAS MY LOCKER?...

SO, DO WE WANT TO SIT IN THE FRONT OF THE CLASS WHERE WE'LL BE PERCEIVED AS NERDS, IN THE BACK WHERE WE'LL BE PERCEIVED AS SLACKERS OR SOMEWHERE IN THE MIDDLE WHERE WE WON'T BE PERCEIVED AS MUCH OF ANYTHING?

C'MON, ASHLEY, LET'S SIT UP FRONT.

CALL ME NERD BOY.

HOW DID WE MAKE DECISIONS BEFORE HORMONES?

HI. I WAS WONDERING IF IT WAS POSSIBLE TO CHANGE SOME OF MY CLASSES.

WHAT SORT OF CHANGES DO YOU HAVE IN MIND?

WELL, YOU'VE GOT ME IN REGULAR ENGLISH AND I'D LIKE TO BE IN THE COLLEGE PREP CLASS... I'M IN ALGEBRA AND I WANT TO MOVE UP TO GEOMETRY... AND I HOPE YOU CAN SOMEHOW GET ME INTO THE 2ND-YEAR FRENCH CLASS.

I'LL SEE WHAT I CAN DO.

I TAKE IT YOU'VE LOOKED INTO THESE CLASSES.

ENOUGH TO SEE ALL THE CUTE BOYS.

AND ISN'T THAT WHAT SCHOOL IS ALL ABOUT?...

I JUST LOVE GETTING A BRAND-NEW TEXTBOOK.

I LOVE MAKING A BOOK-COVER FOR IT OUT OF AN OLD GROCERY BAG... I LOVE THE CRACKING SOUND IT MAKES THE FIRST TIME YOU OPEN IT... I LOVE ALL OF THE CLEAN, CRISP PAGES AND THE WAY IT SMELLS...

AMEND

I LOVE IT! I LOVE IT! I LOVE IT!

LET'S JUST SAY IT WAS A ONE-NIGHT STAND.

I SEE I'LL BE WRITING A CHECK TO THE MATH DEPARTMENT AGAIN...

IT'S FUNNY HOW SUMMER KINDA CLOUDS YOUR MEMORIES.

YOU FORGET HOW ANNOYING MOST OF YOUR FRIENDS ARE.. YOU FORGET HOW HARD IT IS TO WAKE UP FOR SCHOOL... YOU FORGET WHAT A PAIN DOING HOMEWORK REALLY IS..

HUKGACHK!

...YOU FORGET THE IMPORTANCE OF BRINGING A BAG LUNCH...

WHAT **IS** THIS STUFF?!

AMEND

WHAT A WEEK THIS WAS.

I HAD TO READ AN ENTIRE SHAKESPEARE PLAY, WRITE A TWO-PAGE ESSAY ON CRIME, MEMORIZE EVERY ATOMIC SYMBOL AND STAND UP IN CLASS AND DEBATE SOCIAL DARWINISM.

AMEND

AND I'M NOT EVEN GOING TO DISCUSS WHAT I HAD TO DO FOR **MATH**.

WE LEARNED TO PLAY THE AUTOHARP.

WHAT A WEEKEND THIS WILL BE.

THEN WE PLAYED DODGE-BALL...

FoxTrot
BILL AMEND

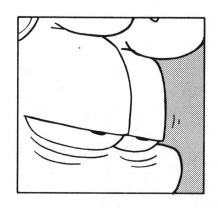

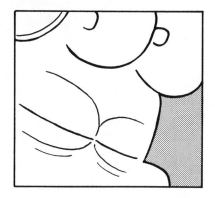

WHERE'S JASON? UPSTAIRS ON THE COMPUTER.

HE TALKED ME INTO SUBSCRIBING TO COMPUNET. IT'S THAT NEW ONLINE INFORMATION SERVICE. HE'S BEEN USING IT ALL AFTERNOON.

IT'S REALLY QUITE REMARKABLE. JASON WAS TELLING ME HOW HE CAN USE IT TO ACCESS THE INTERNET, WHICH WILL CONNECT HIM TO UNIVERSITIES, GOVERNMENT AGENCIES AND PRIVATE COMPUTERS ALL OVER THE WORLD. JUST THINK OF ALL THE FASCINATING THINGS OUR KIDS CAN NOW LEARN!

MISS OCTOBER SURE HAS BIG HOOTERS. I WONDER IF THAT AFFECTS DOWNLOAD TIME...

SO THIS IS THE FAMOUS INTERNET.

THE DATA SUPERHIGHWAY... THE INFORMATION AUTOBAHN... THE BULLET TRAIN TO CYBERVILLE...

COOL.

ACTUALLY, DAD, THE COMPUTER'S NOT TURNED ON. I THOUGHT MAYBE YOU WERE IN A TUNNEL.

WELCOME TO COMPUNET.

YOU HAVE 65,031 WAITING MESSAGES.

MAYBE SETTING MY USERNAME TO "FABIO" WASN'T SUCH A HOT IDEA.

DIANE@ NASA.GOV WISHES TO CHAT. LUCILLE@ OSU.EDU WISHES TO CHAT. JOYCE@ UPS.COM WISHES TO CHAT.

THIS COMPUNET IS REALLY COOL.

NERD.

YOU CAN ACCESS THE INTERNET... NERD.

YOU CAN CHAT WITH FAMOUS CARTOONISTS... NERD.

YOU CAN READ BACK-ISSUE ARTICLES FROM MODEL ROCKETRY MAGAZINE... NERD.

THEY'VE EVEN GOT AN ONLINE MALL WHERE YOU CAN GO SHOPPING.

NERDETTE.

GO FIND OUT WHAT MOM'S CREDIT LIMIT IS.

JASON, WILL YOU PLEASE TURN OFF THE MODEM? I NEED TO USE THE TELEPHONE.

BUT I'M RIGHT IN THE MIDDLE OF A DOWNLOAD!

COMPUNET JUST STARTED CARRYING BLACK BANSHEE COMIC BOOK PREVIEWS. I'M DOWNLOADING THE FIRST THREE PAGES OF NEXT MONTH'S ISSUE.

HOW LONG WILL THAT TAKE?

WELL, LET'S SEE... I STARTED AT ABOUT 4:15...

HOW'S MIDNIGHT SOUND?

JASON, ARE YOU FAMILIAR WITH A LITTLE THING CALLED A PHONE JACK?

JASON, I JUST GOT OUR FIRST COMPUNET BILL.

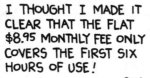

I THOUGHT I MADE IT CLEAR THAT THE FLAT $8.95 MONTHLY FEE ONLY COVERS THE FIRST SIX HOURS OF USE!

SIX HOURS EACH MONTH?! I THOUGHT IT WAS SIX HOURS EACH DAY!

UH-OH...

NOW, THEN, YOUR ALLOWANCE IS ALREADY BEING WITHHELD THROUGH YOUR SOPHOMORE YEAR IN COLLEGE.

IS THIS A BAD TIME TO SUGGEST YOU BUY A FASTER MODEM?

FoxTrot
BILL AMEND

MOM, I DON'T FEEL SO GOOD.

MY STOMACH'S KINDA QUEASY, MY FOREHEAD'S ALL CLAMMY AND MY HEART IS GOING A MILLION BEATS PER SECOND.

I THINK I MAY EVEN THROW UP.

YOU ATE JASON'S CEREAL AGAIN, DIDN'T YOU?

WE WERE OUT OF WHEATIES.

HOW DO YOU SUPPOSE THEY GET GRAIN TO GLOW IN THE DARK?

PETER GETS TO STAY HOME FROM SCHOOL?!

JASON, HE'S SICK.

THAT WONDERFUL GLOW-IN-THE-DARK CEREAL OF YOURS MADE HIM THROW UP.

WHAT?! I EAT TWO BOWLS OF THAT STUFF EVERY DAY AND I HAVEN'T BEEN SICK TO MY STOMACH **ONCE**!

MAYBE I SHOULD BE EATING THREE...

I THINK IT'S TIME I STOPPED TAKING YOU SHOPPING.

I CAN'T BELIEVE ONE BOWL OF CEREAL MADE ME THIS SICK.

WHAT'S IN THIS STUFF, ANYHOW?

I GUESS I SHOULD BE HAPPY IT MADE ME **ONLY** THIS SICK.

NOW AREN'T YOU GLAD YOU TOOK THE **ADVANCED** CHEMISTRY CLASS?

AAAA! MY STOMACH!

AAAA! MY HEAD!

AAAA! MY STOMACH **AND** HEAD!

PEOPLE WHO ARE SICK SHOULD **NOT** WATCH C-SPAN.

CLICK

BRRR... I'M GETTING CHILLS...

NEXT ON "GERALDO": NYMPHOMANIAC LIBRARIANS AND THE BOOKS THAT TURN THEM ON.

(CLICK) NEXT ON "SALLY": THE DIRTY TRUTH BEHIND FEMALE MUD WRESTLING.

(CLICK) NEXT ON "MAURY": PERFORMANCE ART OR GIRLIE STRIP SHOW — YOU DECIDE.

(CLICK) NEXT ON "PHIL": UNIVERSITY WOMEN WHO POSE FOR PLAYBOY.

GOOD LORD — WHAT IS THIS WORLD COMING TO?!

IT'S GOTTEN TO WHERE A FELLOW NEEDS FIVE OR SIX VCRs!

BUT FIRST, THIS MESSAGE FROM MAIDENFORM...

MOM, IT'S INCREDIBLE!

I MEAN, THAT I COULD FEEL SO **SICK** THIS MORNING AND YET FEEL SO **GREAT** RIGHT NOW! IT'S AMAZING!

LOOK AT ME DANCE — I **MUST** BE CURED! HALLELUJAH! O HAPPY DAY!

PETER, IF YOU WERE TOO SICK FOR SCHOOL, YOU'RE TOO SICK FOR THE MOVIES.

BUT MOMMM... "BLOODSPORT VII" OPENS TONIGHT!

YOU KNOW, FOR SOMEONE WHO CLAIMS TO HAVE BEEN QUEASY ALL DAY...

FoxTrot
BILL AMEND

Ocelot

Giant Panda

Gray Wolf

Bengal Tiger

California Condor

Black Rhino

Humpback Whale

Peter Fox

FoxTrot
BILL AMEND

WHAT ARE YOU DOING? I HEARD THAT THE GUY WHO DRAWS "THE FAR SIDE" IS RETIRING AT THE END OF THE YEAR.

GARY LARSON? YEAH, I HEARD THAT TOO. SO? WELL, I FIGURE THAT JUST BECAUSE **HE'S** QUITTING, IT DOESN'T MEAN THAT "THE FAR SIDE" HAS TO END. I'LL JUST TAKE IT OVER FOR HIM. I'M PUTTING TOGETHER A SAMPLE BATCH NOW.

THINK ABOUT IT! OVERNIGHT, YOUR LITTLE BROTHER COULD BECOME ONE OF THE WORLD'S MOST WIDELY READ CARTOONISTS! I'D BE FAMOUS! PEOPLE WOULD BE BEATING A PATH TO OUR DOOR!

WITH PITCHFORKS AND TORCHES, MOST LIKELY. HEE HEE HEE— IF YOU THINK **THAT** ONE'S GROSS...

The Far Side II
by Jason Fox

Dang, Zeke, but that is one ugly cow!

The Far Side II
by Jason Fox

Wait a minute...this can't be Earth — Earth has humans.

FoxTrot
BILL AMEND

HAVE YOU SEEN MY PUMPKIN ANYWHERE?

NO.

HAVE YOU SEEN MY PUMPKIN ANYWHERE?

NO.

HOW COULD I HAVE LOST MY PUMPKIN?! I JUST CARVED IT!

ASK ME IF I'VE SEEN IT.

YOU LIVE FOR THIS WEEK, DON'T YOU?

WHAT ARE YOU DOING?

RIGGING UP SOME ROBOT ZOMBIES FOR THE FRONT YARD.

WHEN THE TRICK-OR-TREATERS BREAK THE INFRA-RED BEAM OUT BY THE MAILBOX, THE TAPE DECK KICKS IN, THE EERIE MUSIC STARTS, AND ONE BY ONE THESE MOTOR-IZED ARMS POP OUT OF THE LAWN. THEN THE FUN REALLY BEGINS.

I SURE HOPE I CAN THROW THESE COW GUTS WITH ACCURACY.

YOU KNOW, THE IDEA ISN'T TO PREVENT KIDS FROM EVEN MAKING IT TO OUR FRONT DOOR... DID YOU SEE ALL THE HUMONGOUS CANDY BARS MOM BOUGHT?!

WHO SUCKED ALL THE FILLING OUT OF THE TWINKIES?!

HURRY, OR WE REALLY WILL NEED COFFINS.

WHOA, PETER! GREAT COSTUME!

I MEAN, HOW DID YOU EVER THINK OF THAT?! — THE LITTLE STEVEN SPIELBERG AND MICHAEL CRICHTON DOLLS ARE A STROKE OF IRONIC GENIUS! IT'S BRILLIANT! IT'S THE BEST HALLOWEEN COSTUME EVER!

I BOW IN HUMBLE AWE, O AMAZING OLDER SIBLING.

I'M NOT PETER. I'M PAIGE.

WHAT'S WITH THE WHITE MAKE-UP? ARE YOU DRESSING UP AS A GHOST?

THIS ISN'T MAKE-UP.

I CAN'T DECIDE WHETHER TO CALL IT "PUMPKINMATION" OR "JACK-O-MATION."

ABOUT THIS PRODUCE BILL...

I JUST DON'T KNOW WHAT I'M GOING TO DO ABOUT HALLOWEEN CANDY THIS YEAR.

HERE IT IS, TWO DAYS BEFORE HALLOWEEN AND THERE ARE NO MORE CHOCOLATE BARS, PEANUT BUTTER CUPS, SWEET-TARTS OR GUMMI WORMS! ALL THAT'S LEFT ARE A FEW RANDOM PACKS OF GUM!

IN THE STORES?

IN OUR CANDY BOWL!

AHH.

WE'RE OUT OF GUM.

FoxTrot

BILL AMEND

FoxTrot
BILL AMEND

I DON'T KNOW WHAT I LIKE BEST ABOUT THIS SHOW.

ITS TWISTING STORY LINES... ITS DIABOLICAL CHARACTERS... ITS HUNKY MALE ACTORS...

AAAA! WHAT ARE YOU WATCHING?!? MONDAY NIGHT FOOTBALL IS ON!

...ITS DRAMATIC POWER...

THAT'D BE MY VOTE.

SUPPOSE I WERE TO PAY YOU KIDS $5 APIECE...

MOM! MOM! LOOK WHAT I GOT FROM MARCUS!

IT'S THE SERIES-B PLASMA-MAN BUBBLE GUM CARD! THIS IS THE ONLY ONE I DIDN'T HAVE! I'VE BEEN TRYING TO GET IT FOR MONTHS!

HE JUST GAVE IT TO YOU?

WELL, NO, I HAD TO TRADE HIM SOMETHING FOR IT.

ANOTHER CARD?

HONESTLY.

IT'S NOT LIKE PAIGE RIDES IT MUCH.

MY STUPID ENGLISH TEACHER HAS LOST HIS MIND!

NOW WHAT?

HE EXPECTS US TO READ THIS FAT 400-PAGE BOOK PRACTICALLY OVERNIGHT!

OUCH. WHEN'S IT DUE? FRIDAY?

UM, NO...

MONDAY?

LOOK, NEVER MIND.

TUESDAY?

I HEAR YOU HAVE TO READ SOME BOOK BY NEW YEAR'S.

FoxTrot
BILL AMEND

MOM, IS IT OK IF I STAY OVER AT NICOLE'S?

PAIGE, NO.

YOU HAVEN'T FINISHED YOUR HOMEWORK... YOUR ROOM IS A MESS... YOU PROMISED YOU'D HELP ME WITH DINNER...

Cartoonist to direct "Jurassic Park II"

BESIDES, TONIGHT IS A SCHOOL NIGHT.

ACTUALLY, I MEANT FOR THE WEEK.

GUESS WHAT MOVIE OPENS IN 5,526 MINUTES...

THE WEEK??

THAT'S ONE DOG-EARED MAGAZINE.

IT'S THE CINEMAFANGIQUE "STAR TREK: GENERATIONS" PREVIEW ISSUE. I READ IT EVERY DAY AFTER SCHOOL.

CINEMAFANGIQUE

IT'S GOT ALL THESE AMAZING BEHIND-THE-SCENES PHOTOS! HERE'S BRENT "DATA" SPINER GETTING HIS HAIR COMBED... HERE'S WORF SITTING IN BEVERLY CRUSHER'S DIRECTOR'S CHAIR... HERE'S PATRICK STEWART EATING A BAGEL BETWEEN SHOTS... I THINK IT'S POPPYSEED...

ISN'T THIS JUST THE COOLEST STUFF YOU'VE EVER SEEN IN YOUR LIFE, DAD?! ISN'T IT?! ISN'T IT?! ISN'T IT?!

I BELIEVE WHAT WE HAVE HERE IS A "STAR TREK: GENERATIONS" GAP.

HERE'S WILLIAM SHATNER TYING HIS SHOES...

PETER! PETER! I DID IT!

SPATS ILLUSTRATED

I MEMORIZED THE ENTIRE KLINGON DICTIONARY! 191 PAGES AND I KNOW IT ALL! I'M GONNA BE THE BEST KLINGON IN THE THEATER FRIDAY, I KNOW IT!

ASK ME SOMETHING! ANYTHING! I KNOW ALL 1,400 WORDS!

WHY??

"QATLH." C'MON— GIMME SOMETHING HARD...

41

MOM, HURRY UP! I DON'T WANT TO BE LATE!

EVERYBODY IN THE UNIVERSE IS GOING TO WANT TO SEE THIS "STAR TREK" MOVIE! IT'S PROBABLY SOLD-OUT ALREADY!

I TOLD MARCUS WE'D PICK HIM UP 10 MINUTES AGO! I'VE GOT YOUR CAR KEYS RIGHT HERE!

JASON, THIS MOVIE DOESN'T OPEN UNTIL TOMORROW.

OOPS— I NEARLY FORGOT MY SLEEPING BAG.

IT'S AMAZING TO ME, JASON, HOW CUTE YOU WERE AS AN INFANT...

CAN I HELP YOU?

I AM KLINGON! I WANT A LARGE TUB OF NARENDIAN GAGH-WORMS!

RAW! WITH EXTRA GAGH BLOOD! AND THEY HAD BETTER BE WIGGLING!

LOOK, KID, IT'S BEEN A REALLY LONG DAY...

OK, GIMME A MEDIUM POPCORN.

WHY CAN'T WE JUST SHOW ART FLICKS?

DO YOUR REPLICATORS MAKE DECENT NACHOS?

GREAT. THE MOVIE EVENT OF A LIFETIME AND WE'RE STUCK BEHIND A COUPLE OF "HOMNS."

DID YOU BRING YOUR PHASER?

FoxTrot
BILL AMEND

MOM, CAN I MAKE DINNER SOMETIME THIS WEEK?

SURE.

HOW 'BOUT THURSDAY? FINE.

THIS'LL BE FUN. I'VE NEVER COOKED A TURKEY BEFORE.

PAIGE, DON'T MAKE TURKEY — WE'RE HAVING IT FOR THANKSGI...

TOO LATE! YOU SAID YES!

GIVE ME THAT COOKBOOK!

THIS IS GOING TO BE THE MOST **AMAZING** THANKSGIVING DINNER THIS FAMILY HAS EVER EXPERIENCED!

I'M GOING TO COOK OURS THE EXACT SAME WAY MARTHA STEWART COOKS HERS.

MARTHA STEWART'S THANKSGIVING

I'LL NEED A NEW WARDROBE.

THE AMAZEMENT BEGINS.

PAIGE, WHAT ARE YOU DOING?

I'M DECORATING THE HOUSE FOR THANKSGIVING.

HARPER'S

I GATHERED A BUNCH OF LEAVES FROM THE YARD. I THOUGHT I'D MAKE A NICE CENTERPIECE, À LA MARTHA STEWART.

PAIGE, THOSE LEAVES ARE PROBABLY CRAWLING WITH BUGS.

HARPER'S

AIEEE!

PAIGE, SWEETIE, THANKSGIVING IS ENOUGH WORK **WITHOUT** YOUR ASSISTANCE.

EEK! NOW THE BUGS ARE ON THE FLOOR!

CRUNCH CRUNCH CRUNCH

FoxTrot
BILL AMEND

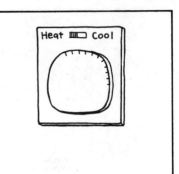

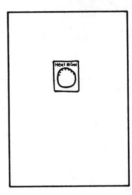

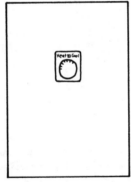

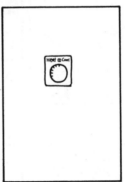

IT'S SNOWING! IT'S SNOWING!

THEY'RE GOING TO CANCEL SCHOOL! THEY'RE GOING TO CANCEL SCHOOL!

I SUPPOSE I SHOULD BE FLATTERED THAT THE UNIVERSE HAS IT OUT FOR ME.

YIPPEE! SCHOOL'S NOT CANCELED!

I DON'T GET IT.

WHAT?

CLICK CLICK CLICK

I PICKED UP THIS RUBIK'S CUBE AT THE NEIGHBOR'S GARAGE SALE. APPARENTLY THIS WAS LIKE **THE** PUZZLE OF THE 1980s.

IT WAS, BELIEVE ME.

IT'S MIND-BOGGLING. I JUST CAN'T FIGURE IT OUT.

HOW TO DO IT?

CLICK CLICK CLICK

HOW PEOPLE COULD THINK THIS WAS **HARD**.

SPEAKING OF THINGS MIND-BOGGLING...

OOF!

UGGH!

MAN!

YOU KNOW, YOU **COULD** MAKE YOUR BAG LUNCHES SMALLER...

CAN YOU GIVE ME A HAND WITH THE DOOR?

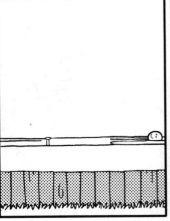

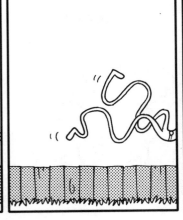

FoxTrot
BILL AMEND

A SUBSTITUTE TEACHER IN ENGLISH...

MARY BEAUTIFUL BRUSHING AGAINST US IN THE HALL...

TACOS FOR LUNCH...

CLEARLY, THERE **IS** A GOD.

AT LEAST UNTIL THE TRIG TEST.

Beep Beep

I'VE GOT TO START COMING HOME AFTER DARK.

WHAT ARE YOU DOING?

OH, WITH THE HOLIDAYS COMING UP, I THOUGHT I'D KNIT MYSELF A LITTLE SOMETHING.

MOM, HERE'S AN ADDENDUM TO MY CHRISTMAS LIST.

MOM, WERE THE COOKIES SUPPOSED TO TURN BLACK LIKE THIS?

MOM, DON'T TELL ME THIS WAS ALL THE EGGNOG YOU BOUGHT.

UM, STRAIT-JACKETS HAVE LONGER SLEEVES.

YOU LAUGH...

FoxTrot
BILL AMEND

YOU MIGHT WANT TO ASK SANTA TO REPLACE A FEW OLD-GROWTH FORESTS WHILE YOU'RE AT IT.

I JUST HOPE HE CAN READ THIS LIST IN TWO WEEKS.

PRINTZZZZ
PRINTZZZZ
PRINTZZZZ
PRINTZZZZ

I DON'T KNOW **WHAT** TO GET YOUR BROTHER JASON FOR CHRISTMAS.

THERE ARE JUST TOO MANY TOYS, TOO MANY VIDEO GAMES TO CHOOSE FROM!

IT'S UNREAL.

DIDN'T HE MAKE A LIST?

I'M TALKING ABOUT HIS LIST.

YOU COULD BUY THE KID SOME SEDATIVES.

BUILDING A SNOWMAN?

NOT JUST **ANY** SNOWMAN.

THIS WILL BE THE BIGGEST, THE HUGEST, THE MOST COLOSSAL SNOWMAN THE WORLD HAS EVER SEEN!

HE DOESN'T **LOOK** VERY BIG.

THIS IS ONE OF HIS MOLECULES.

AH, SILLY ME.

CAN YOU TELL MOM I MIGHT BE A LITTLE LATE FOR DINNER?

Let Set A represent all three-letter words. Let Set B represent all four-letter words.

Let Set C represent all words containing two vowels.

I HATE THESE MICKEY MOUSE PROBLEMS.

IT'S **RIDICULOUS!**

HOW AM I SUPPOSED TO DO ALL THIS HOMEWORK LESS THAN TWO WEEKS BEFORE CHRISTMAS?!

THERE ARE JUST TOO MANY DISTRACTIONS! HOW AM I SUPPOSED TO STAY FOCUSED?! HOW AM I SUPPOSED TO GET MOTIVATED?! HOW AM I SUPPOSED TO EVEN **THINK** ABOUT SCHOOLWORK?!

LET ME GET THIS STRAIGHT — YOU WANT ME TO JUST STAND HERE AND GLARE...

IF YOU DON'T MIND.

HEY, PAIGE, WANNA PLAY BLACKJACK?

OK.

I'LL DEAL. (FLIP FLIP FLIP FLIP) YOU SHOW A FOUR, I SHOW A SEVEN.

HIT ME.

I'M SORRY — MY HEARING MUST BE GOING. WHAT WAS THAT?

I SAID HIT ME.

NOW **THAT'S** WHAT I CALL A CARD GAME.

HEY, JASON, WANNA PLAY **WAR?**

JASON, I APPRECIATE YOUR DESIRE TO HELP DECORATE THE TREE THIS YEAR.

IT'S A FAMILY TRADITION AND IT WARMS MY HEART TO SEE YOU SO EAGERLY JOINING IN.

BUT SWEETIE...

I KNEW THERE'D BE A "BUT"...

DON'T YOU THINK PLASTIC SKELETONS ARE MORE APPROPRIATE FOR HALLOWEEN?

BUT THEY GLOW IN THE DARK! YOU WON'T HAVE TO MESS WITH LIGHTS!

FoxTrot
BILL AMEND

Panel 1: WELL, ANDY, YOU'LL BE PLEASED TO KNOW I'M NOT GOING TO GO CRAZY DECORATING THE HOUSE THIS CHRISTMAS.

Panel 2: EVERY YEAR I TRY TO OUTDO THE NEIGHBORS, AND EVERY YEAR I END UP NEARLY ELECTROCUTING MYSELF IN THE PROCESS. THERE COMES A POINT WHERE A MAN JUST HAS TO RECOGNIZE HIS OWN LIMITATIONS.

Panel 3: SO... NO MORE FANCY LIGHTING SCHEMES FOR **THIS** HOMEOWNER. NO SIRREE.

WHY, ROGER, I DO BELIEVE YOU'RE SHOWING SIGNS OF SANITY IN YOUR OLD AGE.

Panel 4: I'M LETTING JASON DO IT.

AS USUAL, I SPOKE TOO SOON.

I ASSUME YOU'D LIKE TO KEEP THE COST UNDER FIVE FIGURES, IF POSSIBLE.

Panel 5: WHAT'S WITH ALL THE MAGAZINES?

I'M TRYING TO FIGURE OUT HOW I WANT TO LIGHT OUR HOUSE FOR CHRISTMAS.

Panel 6: I'M GOING THROUGH THESE TRAVEL MAGAZINES LOOKING FOR INSPIRATIONAL PHOTOS.

Nonde Cast

Panel 7: OF COZY NEW ENGLAND HAMLETS?

OF THE LAS VEGAS STRIP.

Panel 8: AH, TO BE THE FIRST HOUSE ON OUR BLOCK WITH NEON.

MOVING NEON.

Panel 9: WHAT ARE YOU DOING?

DRAWING UP PRELIMINARY SKETCHES OF HOW I'M GOING TO DECORATE OUR YARD FOR CHRISTMAS.

Panel 10: IT'S IMPORTANT TO BEGIN WITH A UNIFYING THEME TO TIE EVERYTHING TOGETHER, BUT I CAN'T DECIDE WHICH IDEA I LIKE BEST.

Panel 11: I STARTED OFF THINKING I'D DO A STANDARD SANTA'S VILLAGE, BUT THEN I THOUGHT OF DOING ONE A BIT MORE PIRATE-ORIENTED. THEN I HAD THIS GREAT IDEA: A **JURASSIC** CHRISTMAS. WHAT DO YOU THINK?

Panel 12: I THINK THESE PENS' FUMES MUST PACK QUITE A WALLOP.

STILL, I LIKE THE IDEA OF SANTA SAYING YO HO HO..

FoxTrot
BILL AMEND

WHAT ARE YOU DOING?

TRYING TO COME UP WITH A GOOD NEW YEAR'S RESOLUTION.

I WANT SOMETHING SIGNIFICANT, YET DOABLE. I TAKE THESE VOWS SERIOUSLY.

WHAT'D YOU RESOLVE LAST YEAR?

NOT TO PROCRASTINATE SO MUCH.

AHH.

OH, WHAT THE HECK. I STILL HAVE FIVE DAYS TO DO THIS.

HAVE **YOU** THOUGHT OF A NEW YEAR'S RESOLUTION?

ACTUALLY, YES, I HAVE.

I'M RESOLVING TO BE YOUR NEW BEST FRIEND. BEGINNING SUNDAY, WE'LL BE INSEPARABLE. WHEN YOU WATCH TV, **I'LL** WATCH TV. WHEN YOU GO TO THE MALL, **I'LL** GO TO THE MALL.

IF YOU EVEN **THINK** OF FOLLOWING ME TO THE MALL...

...AND WHEN YOU SAY THINGS LIKE THAT, I'LL JUST SAY, "I LOVE YOU, SIS."

AAAAAAAAAAAAA!

I THOUGHT YOUR RESOLUTION WAS TO DRIVE PAIGE NUTS.

SO I STARTED A LITTLE EARLY.

PETER, DO YOU MAKE NEW YEAR'S RESOLUTIONS?

NOPE.

HOW COME?

IT JUST SEEMS KINDA POINTLESS. YOU START OUT WITH ALL THESE HIGH HOPES AND EXPECTATIONS, BUT THEN EVENTUALLY REALITY SETS IN AND IT ALL GOES OUT THE WINDOW.

THEN YOU FEEL DEPRESSED UNTIL THE **NEXT** YEAR, WHEN YOU BASICALLY DO THE EXACT SAME THING ALL OVER AGAIN. IT'S AN ENDLESS CYCLE OF FAILURE. WHY BOTHER?!

THIS FROM A DIE-HARD RED SOX FAN.

HEY, THEY'RE WINNING IT **ALL** THIS YEAR— YOU **WATCH**..

59

FoxTrot
BILL AMEND

I CAN'T BELIEVE TODAY'S REALLY A HOLIDAY.

I CAN'T BELIEVE I REALLY DON'T HAVE TO GO TO WORK.

MOM! JASON'S SHOOTING FROOT LOOPS OUT OF HIS NOSE!

BLASTED CALENDAR.

JASON, GIVE ME THAT CEREAL!

PAIGE STARTED IT.

DID NOT!

DID TOO.

OW!

MOM, CAN I TAKE THE CAR TO DENISE'S HOUSE? SHE INVITED ME OVER FOR LUNCH.

THAT'S FINE. WHEN WILL YOU BE HOME?

PROBABLY SOMETIME AROUND 2:00.

AHEM.

...P.M.

HAVE FUN.

THE CURSE OF THE PARANOID MOTHER...

UM, MOM? MY SOUP KINDA EXPLODED IN THE MICROWAVE.

HOW DID **THAT** HAPPEN?!

I DON'T KNOW.

DID YOU FOLLOW THE INSTRUCTIONS?

I FORGET.

WELL, LET'S FIND OUT. WHERE'S THE CAN?

I TOLD YOU, IT EXPLODED.

PAIGE, DIDN'T WE GO THROUGH THIS WITH OUR **FIRST** MICROWAVE?

WHAT ARE YOU DOING? WRITING A COMPUTER PROGRAM TO DETERMINE THE IDEAL SNOWBALL.

I WANT TO MAXIMIZE RANGE, ACCURACY AND IMPACT DAMAGE WHILE MINIMIZING ARM FATIGUE AND PACKING TIME. IT'S A CHALLENGING PROBLEM.

STILL, KNOWING THE PERFECT SIZE, SHAPE AND MASS IS JUST THE SORT OF EDGE I CAN EXPLOIT THE NEXT TIME PAIGE COMES NEAR MY SNOW FORT. HEE HEE HEE.

MEANTIME IT'S SPRING... GOOD POINT. I PROBABLY SHOULD ACCOUNT FOR AIR TEMPERATURE.

I'M TELLING YOU, MOM, "THE X-FILES" IS THE COOLEST SHOW ON TV.

NOT JUST ONCE IN A WHILE, EITHER. EVERY EPISODE IS COOL, START TO FINISH. TOTALLY. FULLY. BIG-TIME.

AND I KNOW COOL. ARE THESE LT. WORF UNDERPANTS YOURS?

STEVE YOUNG FADES BACK TO PASS!

HE SPOTS AN OPEN JERRY RICE STREAKING DOWNFIELD!

ACTUALLY, DAD, MAYBE WE SHOULD JUST STICK TO HANDOFFS. (OOF) STUPID POSTSEASON...

63

FoxTrot
BILL AMEND

JASON MUST HAVE SOME BIG HOMEWORK ASSIGNMENT DUE TOMORROW.

WHY DO YOU SAY THAT?

HE'S HAD HIS NOSE BURIED IN EITHER A DICTIONARY OR A THESAURUS FOR MOST OF THE EVENING.

Cartoonist sets Land Speed Record

I MEAN, I CAN'T IMAGINE A NORMAL KID JUST DOING THAT FOR FUN.

THE KEY WORD, ROGER, IS "NORMAL".

HAS ANYONE EVER TOLD YOU THAT YOUR CORPULENCE IS DOWNRIGHT BROBDINGNAGIAN?

DR. TING?

YES, PAIGE?

ABOUT FRIDAY'S TEST— DOES IT COVER ALL OF CHAPTER FOUR AND PART OF CHAPTER FIVE, OR PART OF CHAPTER FOUR AND ALL OF CHAPTER FIVE?

HI, BOBBY! I LIKE YOUR SWEATER!

IT COVERS CHAPTERS 11 AND 12.

I'M SORRY, WHAT WAS THAT?

BY THE WAY, THE TEST IS ON THURSDAY.

I AM SO FULL.

I DEFINITELY ATE TOO MUCH.

I THINK I'M GOING TO EXPLODE.

SO WHAT'S FOR DESSERT?

65

HEY, MOM, LOOK! I GOT AN "A-" ON MY HISTORY ASSIGNMENT!

PETER, GOOD FOR YOU!

WE HAD TO LIST 10 GREAT AMERICANS AND WRITE A PARAGRAPH ABOUT EACH ONE.

I HAD JEFFERSON, FRANKLIN, KING, LINCOLN... IT WAS THE PERFECT LIST.

SO WHY AN A-MINUS?

APPARENTLY "GREAT" IS A RELATIVE TERM.

YOU INCLUDED YOURSELF?!

POW!

UM, WITHOUT ADMITTING ANYTHING, I BELIEVE THAT'S MY MITTEN.

SUCH PRETTY LITTLE TEETH...

WHY ARE YOU IN YOUR PAJAMAS?

I'M GOING TO BED.

NOW?! I KNOW IT'S EARLY, BUT I FIGURE THE SOONER I GO TO BED, THE SOONER IT'LL BE TOMORROW MORNING. AND WE ALL KNOW WHAT TOMORROW IS...

SUPER BOWL SUNDAY!

AT LEAST EAT SOME LUNCH FIRST.

I JUST WISH I WERE TIRED.

FoxTrot
BILL AMEND

RUNNING SHOES...

OVERCOAT...

IGUANA.

MOTH-ERRR!

HOW TO REALLY DRESS FOR SUCCESS.

AMEND

GREETINGS. I AM IGUANOMAN.

JASON, YOU ARE SO WEIRD.

I COME FROM A GALAXY FAR, FAR AWAY, BUT I SEEM TO HAVE MADE A WRONG TURN SOMEWHERE.

COULD YOU POSSIBLY DIRECT ME TO THE PLANET EARTH?

THIS IS EARTH, YOU GEEK!

AMEND

RIGHT. AND I SUPPOSE YOU'RE GOING TO TELL ME YOU'RE HUMAN.

ACTUALLY, I'M ON THE VERGE OF GOING APE.

GREETINGS, EARTHLING. WHAT'S FOR DINNER?

ZITI NEFERTITI.

WHAT'S THAT?

OH, JUST A LITTLE SOMETHING I MADE UP. IT'S PASTA TUBES STUFFED WITH MASHED EGGPLANT AND GREEN OLIVES.

I WAS AFRAID OF THIS. MY DIGESTIVE TRACT IS INCOMPATIBLE WITH YOUR HUMANOID DIET. I WILL REQUIRE ALTERNATIVE SUSTENANCE.

SUCH AS?

AMEND

I BELIEVE YOU EARTHLINGS CALL THEM "HO HO'S."

JASON, MUST WE GO THROUGH THIS EVERY OTHER DAY?

JASON, WILL YOU GET **LOST**?!

I TOLD YOU, I AM NOT JASON. I AM IGUANOMAN.

FINE. IGUANO-MAN, WILL YOU GET **LOST**?!

YOUR TONE OF DISRESPECT IS A SURE WAY TO LAND YOURSELF A SLAVE JOB IN ONE OF MY PLANET'S CRICKET MINES. I DEMAND AN APOLOGY.

AND THOSE NACHOS.

DOES MOLTEN CHEESE STAIN?

ORDINARILY, I'D ASK "HOW"...

WELL, WELL, WHAT HAVE WE HERE?

I AM IGUANOMAN. YOU MUST BE THE ONE THEY CALL "DAD."

THAT WOULD BE ME.

I HAVE TRAVELED LIGHT-YEARS THROUGH SPACE TO BRING YOU A MESSAGE FROM MY SUPREME COMMANDER, IGUANIUS THE ALMIGHTY.

AND WHAT MIGHT THAT MESSAGE BE?

"INCREASE JASON FOX'S ALLOWANCE OR WE WILL DESTROY YOUR PLANET."

SON, WOULD YOU **LIKE** YOUR FATHER TO START HITTING BARS ON THE WAY HOME FROM WORK?

NOW, GIVEN THAT THE EARTH IS PROBABLY WORTH A FEW QUADRILLION DOLLARS...

STUPID PHYSICS.

WHY DO YOU SAY THAT?

I WANT TO GO BACK TO MY PLANET FOR LUNCH, BUT TRAVELING AT THE SPEEDS I DO, RELATIVITY THEORY TELLS ME THAT YOU ALL WILL HAVE AGED THOUSANDS OF YEARS BY THE TIME I RETURN. YOU'LL BE NOTHING BUT DUST BY THEN.

WHAT A PITY.

THAT WE WON'T MEET AGAIN?

THAT I WON'T GET TO WATCH YOU SHRIVEL UP.

JASON, I WOULDN'T BE SO SURE **YOU'LL** BE OUTLIVING **ME**...

FoxTrot
BILL AMEND

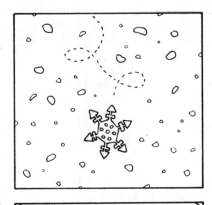

OW!

YOU KNOW HOW THEY SAY NO TWO SNOWFLAKES ARE ALIKE?

IS THIS SOMETHING THEY CAN **PROVE**, OR IS IT JUST SOME OLD WIVES' TALE KIND OF THING?

I MEAN, THERE MUST BE **TRILLIONS** OF SNOWFLAKES FALLING AROUND THE WORLD RIGHT NOW.

AND ARE YOU ALLOWED TO COMPARE PRESENT SNOWFLAKES WITH PAST ONES? BECAUSE THEN YOU'D HAVE TO INCLUDE ALL THE ZILLIONS OF SNOWFLAKES THAT HAVE FALLEN IN THE EARTH'S 4.6 BILLION-YEAR HISTORY.

THAT'S A LOT.

AND WHAT ABOUT SNOWFLAKES THAT MIGHT FALL ON OTHER PLANETS? DO WE GET TO COMPARE THOSE TOO? EVENTUALLY THERE'D **HAVE** TO BE DUPLICATES.'

OF COURSE, IF THEY'RE TALKING ABOUT BEING THE SAME RIGHT DOWN TO EACH ATOM, THE HEISENBERG UNCERTAINTY PRINCIPLE WOULD MAKE EXACT COMPARISONS CONVENIENTLY IMPOSSIBLE.

HMMM...

AMEND

I WONDER IF PHILOSOPHERS DIE MORE OFTEN IN THE WINTER.

AND WHAT ABOUT MAN-MADE SNOWFLAKES?

Panel 1: ANDY, I'VE GOT A LOT OF WORK ON MY DESK I NEED TO CATCH UP ON.

Panel 2: I'D LIKE TO STAY HERE AT THE OFFICE A WHILE LONGER, IF THAT'S OK. WHEN WILL YOU BE HOME?

Panel 3: PROBABLY AROUND 9:00. ROGER, THIS IS THE THIRD STRAIGHT WEEK YOU'VE DONE THIS.

Panel 4: SINCE WHEN ARE MONDAYS SO AWFUL? "MELROSE"!~ "VOYAGER"!~ "MELROSE"!~ "VOYAGER"!~ "MELROSE"!~ LET GO!~ OW!~

Panel 5: IT'S UNBELIEVABLE HOW MUCH HOMEWORK I HAVE TO DO TONIGHT!

Panel 6: I CAN'T REMEMBER THE LAST TIME I HAD THIS MANY THINGS DUE!

Panel 7: I DON'T KNOW **WHAT** ALL MY TEACHERS WERE THINKING! IN THAT CASE, SWEETIE, WHY DON'T **I** DO THE DISHES?

Panel 8: I THOUGHT YOU HAD **NO** HOMEWORK... IT'S ALL IN HOW YOU SAY IT.

Panel 9: JASON WAS SO DARLING THIS MORNING. OH?

Panel 10: HE WANTED TO KNOW IF HE COULD BRING THAT CUTE PICTURE OF PAIGE TO SCHOOL FOR HIS CLASSMATES TO SEE. I WONDER WHAT FOR.

Panel 11: I ASSUME BECAUSE HE WANTS TO SHOW OFF HIS SISTER. WHAT OTHER REASON COULD THERE BE?

Panel 12: ...AND TO CONCLUDE MY REPORT, I OFFER PHOTOGRAPHIC **PROOF** OF THE SASQUATCH! THANK YOU, JASON. YOU CAN SIT DOWN NOW.

Farmer Bob's field measures 150 yards by 250 yards.

He wants to use 60 percent of his land for growing brussels sprouts, 30 percent for lima beans, and 10 percent for cauliflower.

What is the square footage he'll need to allocate for each crop?

LIKE I'M REALLY GONNA LIFT A FINGER TO HELP THIS GUY.

GLUG GLUG GLUG GLUG GLUG

WHERE'S PAIGE?? WHERE'S PAIGE?? WHERE'S PAIGE??

UPSTAIRS, I THINK.

BRAAAP!

TOO LATE. NEVER MIND.

PETER, WHY DON'T YOU GO UPSTAIRS ANYWAY.

PAIGE, YOU KNOW YOUR MOTHER PRETTY WELL. WHAT DO **YOU** THINK I SHOULD GET HER FOR VALENTINE'S DAY?

CHOCOLATES. ONE OF THOSE REALLY BIG, HEART-SHAPED BOXES. WITH LOTS OF COCONUT ONES.

BUT YOUR MOTHER'S ON A DIET.

I'M NOT.

PETER, YOU KNOW YOUR MOTHER PRETTY WELL...

OK, FINE. **FLOWERS** AND CHOCOLATES.

FoxTrot
BILL AMEND

The Drama Club Announces Open Auditions For **ANTONY** and **CLEOPATRA** All this week 3PM in the Auditorium

STRANGE... I SUDDENLY FEEL AS THOUGH I'M BEING TUGGED BY AN OVERWHELMING FORCE.

THAT'D BE ME SAYING WE'RE GONNA BE LATE FOR CLASS. NO, NO—IT'S A **NEW** SORT OF TUGGING.

HI. I'M HERE TO AUDITION FOR "ANTONY AND CLEOPATRA." GREAT. HERE'S A COPY OF THE PLAY. WE'LL BE STARTING IN A MINUTE.

SAY, YOU LOOK REALLY FAMILIAR. HAVE WE MET?

DIDN'T I SEE YOU IN "STREETCAR" LAST SUMMER?

ACTUALLY, I TRY TO AVOID PUBLIC TRANSPORTATION. OOO—AN IMPROV TYPE. I **LIKE** THIS GIRL!

UM, I'M NOT SURE WHAT PART I SHOULD BE TRYING OUT FOR. DON'T WORRY ABOUT CASTING, PAIGE. THAT'S MY JOB.

YOU JUST READ THE LINES I'VE HIGHLIGHTED AND WE'LL FIGURE OUT WHERE TO PUT YOU.

"MY DEFECATION DOES BEGIN TO MAKE A BETTER LIFE. 'TIS PALTRY TO BE CAESAR."

OOPS—I MEAN "DESOLATION." THIS MIGHT BE A GOOD TIME TO MENTION THAT WE **ARE** ALSO LOOKING FOR STAGE HANDS.

STEVE SAYS HE SAW YOU AUDITIONING FOR SOME PLAY AFTER SCHOOL. "ANTONY AND CLEOPATRA." SO?

DID YOU MAKE IT?

DON'T KNOW. THEY'LL ANNOUNCE ALL THE CASTING DECISIONS AT THE END OF THE WEEK.

MEANTIME, I CAN'T TELL YOU HOW SCARED I AM.

THAT YOU WON'T GET A PART?

NO, THAT I ACTUALLY MIGHT.

YOU REALLY WANT ME TO PLAY CLEOPATRA?!

ABSOLUTELY, PAIGE. I THINK YOU'LL BE GREAT.

THIS IS INCREDIBLE! I NEVER WOULD HAVE DREAMED THIS WAS POSSIBLE!

ALL MY LIFE I'VE FELT JINXED! ALL MY LIFE I'VE FELT UNLUCKY! FINALLY, FINALLY, THAT'S ALL TURNED AROUND!

SO WHO'S PLAYING ANTONY?

I BELIEVE YOU KNOW MORTON.

MY QUEEN...

YES, PAIGE?

FRITZ, I JUST NOTICED THAT THIS PLAY WAS WRITTEN BY SHAKESPEARE.

THE BARD HIMSELF.

IS IT OK IF I JUST USE THE CLIFFS NOTES?

THIS GIRL JUST KEEPS CRACKING ME UP!

NO, SERIOUSLY...

FoxTrot
BILL AMEND

AHHH...

THERE'S NOTHING LIKE THE SMELL OF SUGAR IN THE MORNING.

THIS IS GOING TO BE GOOD.

WHAT IS?

EATING THIS BOWL OF HONEY CHUNKBERRIES CEREAL.

BLECH.

SEE, THE PROBLEM WITH HONEY CHUNKBERRIES IS THAT, WHILE THEY HAVE THE BEST FLAVOR, THEY GO **SOGGY** SO DARN FAST.

...BUT NOT **THESE** BABIES.

WHY'S THAT?

I DUMPED OUT THE BOX AND LET THEM SOAK OVERNIGHT IN A SPECIAL SUGAR-BASED RESIN I COOKED UP WITH MARCUS. THERE'S NO WAY MILK CAN PENETRATE THIS COATING.

FACE THE FACTS — YOUR BROTHER IS A GENIUS.

KRNCH! KRNCH! KRNCH!

ACTUALLY, THEY **DO** SOUND CRUNCHIER.

UNFORTUNATELY, THOSE WERE MY TEETH.

YOU'RE RIGHT. THIS **IS** GOOD.

AMEND

OK, ANTONY, YOU'VE JUST BEEN TOLD THAT CLEOPATRA HAS KILLED HERSELF AND THE ANGUISH CAUSES YOU TO THROW YOURSELF UPON YOUR OWN SWORD.

TELL YOU WHAT—LET'S USE YOUR DAGGER INSTEAD.

I THINK THAT WAS MY DAGGER.

ABOUT THIS PLAY BEING A TRAGEDY...!

PAIGE, LET'S TRY A RUN-THROUGH OF CLEOPATRA'S DEATH SCENE.

OK.

HERE'S YOUR SNAKE.

SNAKE?! YOU WANT ME TO HOLD A SNAKE?! AAAA! GET IT AWAY FROM ME! AAAA!

GET IT AWAY!

WHAM! WHAM! WHAM!

I SAID CLEOPATRA'S DEATH, NOT THE PROP BOY'S.

HE COULD HAVE TOLD ME THE THING WAS RUBBER...!

OW...

OK, LISTEN UP, PEOPLE.

TOMORROW IS OPENING NIGHT, AND I WANT TO MAKE ONE THING PERFECTLY CLEAR...

THINGS MAY GO WRONG. SOMEONE MAY FORGET A LINE. THAT'S THEATER. BUT REMEMBER, THE SHOW MUST GO ON! I DON'T WANT TO SEE ANY OF YOU CRYING OR PANICKING OR FALLING APART AT THE SEAMS.

...THAT'S MY JOB.

IF WE SEE SOMEONE WE KNOW IN THE AUDIENCE, IS IT OK TO WAVE?

FoxTrot
BILL AMEND

WELL, MOM, I'VE FIGURED OUT WHAT I REALLY WANT TO BE WHEN I GROW UP.

OH?

A FEDERAL AGENT IN THE X-FILES DIVISION. JUST LIKE FOX MULDER ON TV.

THINK ABOUT IT — TRACKING DOWN UFOs, VAMPIRES, SEWER-SWIMMING LAMPREY-MEN... IT'S THE PERFECT JOB FOR SOMEONE LIKE ME — SOMEONE WILLING TO SEE FACT WHERE OTHERS SEE FICTION.

THAT CERTAINLY IS A TALENT OF YOURS.

I WONDER IF I SHOULD TRY TO REACH AGENT MULDER BY PHONE...

HELLO, FBI? I WAS WONDERING IF YOU COULD SEND ME SOME INFORMATION ABOUT BECOMING AN X-FILES AGENT.

YOU KNOW, LIKE IN THE TV SHOW. THE PEOPLE WHO INVESTIGATE THINGS LIKE UFOs AND ALIEN ENCOUNTERS AND —... HELLO? HELLO, ARE YOU THERE?

THEY KEEP HANGING UP ON ME.

DARNED CONSPIRACY OF SILENCE.

JASON, YOU GEEK — THERE'S NO SUCH THING AS THE X-FILES! IT'S JUST A TV SHOW!

YEAH, RIGHT.

THAT'S JUST THE SORT OF THING THIS GUY SAID ABOUT THESE ANCIENT GLOW-IN-THE-DARK BUGS RIGHT BEFORE THEY CAME AND DEVOURED HIM.

EWW.

EXACTLY. SO DON'T BE SO QUICK TO DOUBT THINGS.

SO WHERE'D YOU HEAR ABOUT THIS GUY AND THE BUGS?

ON "THE X-FILES."

Panel 1:

I THOUGHT OF YET ANOTHER REASON WHY I'D BE A PERFECT ADDITION TO THE X-FILES TEAM.

WHICH IS?

Panel 2:

AGENT MULDER'S FIRST NAME IS THE SAME AS MY LAST NAME. THAT MEANS THAT IF AGENT SCULLY WERE IN TROUBLE, SHE'D ONLY HAVE TO YELL "FOX" TO HAVE US BOTH COME RUNNING.

Panel 3:

YEAH, BUT IF SHE SAYS, "FOX, YOU PINHEAD, YOU SCREWED UP AGAIN," THE WRONG FOX MIGHT TAKE OFFENSE.

Panel 4:

AT LEAST YOU'D BE WORKING WITH PEOPLE ACCUSTOMED TO THE UNREAL...

NO, I WOULDN'T.

Panel 5:

I'M GOING DOWN INTO THE BASEMENT TO CHECK FOR SUPERNATURAL ACTIVITY.

X-Files agent-in-training

Panel 6:

IF ANYONE WANTS TO COME LOOK WITH ME, THEY'RE MORE THAN WELCOME.

X-Files agent-in-training

Panel 7:

PETER?... PAIGE?... ANYBODY?...

X-Files agent-in-training

Panel 8:

WHY IS IT THAT BASEMENTS ARE ALWAYS SCARIEST WHEN YOU LEAST WANT THEM TO BE?

MORE THAN GHOSTS, I'D WORRY ABOUT PAIGE LOCKING YOU DOWN THERE.

BLAB-BER-MOUTH.

X-Files agent-in-training

Panel 9:

I'M NEVER GOING TO MAKE IT AS AN X-FILES AGENT AT THIS RATE.

HOW'S THAT?

Panel 10:

I COMBED THE ENTIRE HOUSE AND COULDN'T FIND ONE LOUSY PARANORMAL OCCURRENCE.

Panel 11:

NO GHOSTS... NO VAMPIRES... NO ALIEN BEINGS... NO BIGFOOTS... NO ZOMBIES... NO DISEMBODIED HEADS... NO LAMPREY-MEN COMING OUT OF THE TOILET...

Panel 12:

SOMETIMES I HAVE THE WORST LUCK.

MIGHT I SUGGEST AN ALTERNATIVE POINT OF VIEW?

FoxTrot
BILL AMEND

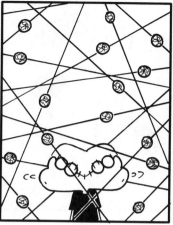

BLECCH!

AAACKH!

HONGXH!

AH, THE IRONY OF HEALTH FOOD.

MEDIC...

IF PETER DIES, CAN I HAVE HIS DESSERT?

WOW!

THAT **IS** INCREDIBLE!

I KNOW **I** WOULD!...

ROGER, I SAID STOP WATCHING THOSE INFOMERCIALS!

DADDY, I'M ON THE PHONE.

IT WOULD APPEAR MY "DRIBBLE UMBRELLA" GAG DIDN'T GO OVER TOO WELL...

FoxTrot
BILL AMEND

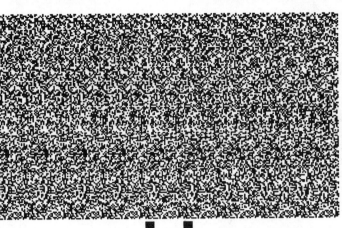

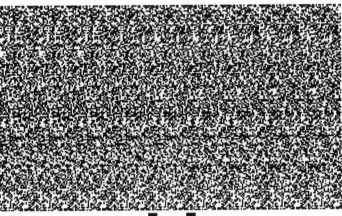

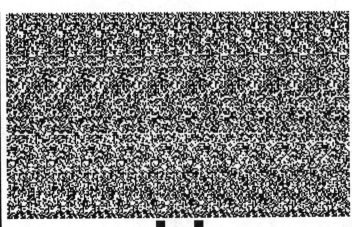

Bottom: DO JASON'S BIDDING

Middle: GIVE JASON MONEY

Top: BOW AND WORSHIP JASON

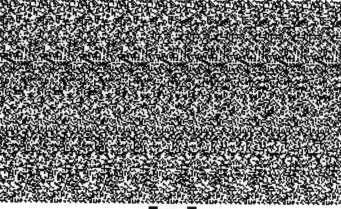

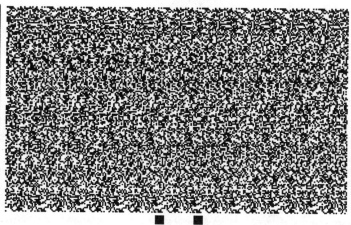

Top: BAKE JASON FOX

Middle: BUY JASON A FERRARI

Bottom: JASON IS YOUR BEST FRIEND

FoxTrot
BILL AMEND

WELCOME TO CNN'S CONTINUING COVERAGE OF THE O.J. SIMPSON TRIAL.

IN JUST A FEW MINUTES, COURT WILL RESUME AND—...

HOLD ON. THIS WAS JUST HANDED TO ME: "A SPACE-CRAFT OF SOME SORT HAS JUST TOUCHED DOWN OUTSIDE U.N. HEADQUARTERS IN NEW YORK. A SMALLISH FIGURE HAS EMERGED AND IS ADDRESSING THE CROWD."
HOLY COW.

NOW, THEN, BACK TO THE TRIAL...

I'M BEGINNING TO SEE WHY ELVIS SHOT THAT TV.

IS Paige Fox a Ferengi?

You decide.

JASON, DID YOU DO THIS?!

YES! YES! YES! YES! YES! YES! YES!

I'VE REALLY GOT TO STOP TAKING SUCH PRIDE IN MY WORK.

WHAT ARE YOU DOING?

THIS EXTRA-CREDIT MATH PROBLEM. IT'S GOT ME TOTALLY STUMPED.

"BOBBY IS DRIVING TO HIS GRANDMOTHER'S HOUSE. IF HE DRIVES THE FIRST HALF OF THE DISTANCE AT AN AVERAGE SPEED OF 20mph, HOW FAST MUST HE DRIVE THE SECOND HALF IN ORDER TO AVERAGE 40 mph FOR THE ENTIRE DISTANCE?"

FOR $5, I'LL TELL YOU THE ANSWER.

NO WAY COULD YOU DO IT— IT'S IMPOSSIBLE!

OF ALL THE LUCKY GUESSES.

AHHH...

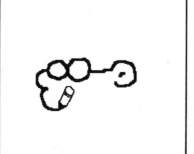

MOM, YOU LOOK AWFUL.

I KNOW.

(SNIFF) IT'S THIS DARN HAY FEVER.

HONK!

ACTUALLY, I MEANT THAT SWEATER-SKIRT COMBINATION.

PAIGE, DON'T YOU HAVE HOMEWORK TO DO?

I CAN'T DECIDE WHAT I HATE MOST ABOUT HAY FEVER.

THE RUNNY NOSE... THE ITCHY EYES... THE ENDLESS SNEEZING...

PBBBTH!

AH, THE SWEET, SWEET SMELL OF SPRING!

...OR THE FACT THAT SOME PEOPLE DON'T GET IT.

WHY DON'T I GO GET YOU SOME MORE KLEENEX.

WELL, TODAY I'VE CLEANED THE HOUSE...

DONE THE SHOPPING... PAID THE BILLS... REORGANIZED THE ATTIC... AND WRITTEN MOST OF NEXT YEAR'S CHRISTMAS CARDS.

AND IT'S NOT YET NOON.

THEY OUGHT TO WARN YOU ABOUT TAKING THESE ANTIHISTAMINES WITH COFFEE.

I DING MA HEH FEFFER ES GEDDIG WUSS.

HUH?

I TED I DING MA HEH FEFFER ED GEDDIG WUDTH.

HUH??

AH DED AH DIGG MA HEH FEFFER ETH GEBBIG WODTH!

I HATE TO SAY THIS, BUT I THINK YOUR HAY FEVER IS GETTING WORSE.

I'B GOIG BAG DO BED.

ROGER, YOU KNEW I HAD ALLERGIES WHEN WE GOT MARRIED!

UM, ANY IDEA WHERE MY SLIPPERS WOULD BE?

WOW. I DON'T THINK I'VE EVER HAD HAY FEVER THAT BAD BEFORE.

THE SNEEZING... THE TEARY EYES... THE CONSTANT NOSE-BLOWING... LORD ONLY KNOWS HOW MANY TISSUES I WENT THROUGH THIS WEEK.

2,036. I WAS OFF BY 300.

HUH?

OH, WAIT— DAD, WAS THE POOL SUPPOSED TO BE SECRET?

AM I THE ONLY ONE WHO VALUES HIS OR HER TIME AROUND HERE?!

FoxTrot
BILL AMEND

94

WHERE'S PETER BEEN ALL EVENING?

UP IN HIS ROOM STUDYING GENETICS.

WHAT FOR?

HE'S THINKING ABOUT TAKING THE SATs NEXT MONTH.

Cartoonist to Captain Seawolf submarine

THEY DON'T HAVE GENETICS QUESTIONS ON THE SATs.

THEN WHAT DO YOU SUPPOSE HE—

SO IF MOM DID WELL ON VERBAL BUT DAD DID REALLY CRUMMY...

EEGAD! I'VE GOT DAD'S HAIR COLOR!

Genetics Made E-Z

0110100011010100I0
10110100110100101101
1001000110111011010I1
0010111011101010I1010
10001100010011011100
0111001011001001110I1

I THOUGHT WE AGREED, NO MORE INTERNET ON SCHOOL NIGHTS.

HEH HEH... HOW'D YOU KNOW?

...AND I THINK THAT BY CONSOLIDATING OUR—...

THUMP!

OUR...

THUMP!

CONSOLIDATING OUR—...

THUMP!
THUMP!
THUMP!
THUMP!
THUMP!
THUMP!
THUMP!
THUMP!

PEOPLE, MAYBE WE OUGHT TO CONSIDER HOLDING THESE MEETINGS BEFORE LUNCH.

THUMP!

ZZZZZZZ

YOU KNOW YOU'VE MADE IT RIGHT WHEN THE **FUMES** WAKE YOU UP.

WHY AM I ON A DESERT ISLAND?

WHY ARE THE COCONUT SHELLS MADE OF CHOCOLATE?

WHY IS HUNKY JIMMY ANDREWS JET-SKIING TOWARD SHORE?

NO, PAIGE, Y IS $\frac{1}{2}X^2$.

ZZZZ... WHY DO I HEAR MY MATH TEACHER'S VOICE?

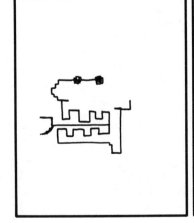

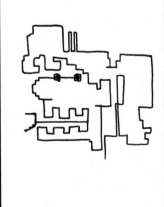

PAIGE IS A

HOW COME EVERY TIME I SEE YOU, YOU'RE SHAKING YOUR ETCH-A-SKETCH?

UM...

FoxTrot
BILL AMEND

UM, JASON? YOU DIDN'T REALLY WANT THAT SECRET DECODER RING, DID YOU?

YOU ATE ANOTHER ONE?!

MOM, I'VE GOT GOOD NEWS AND BAD NEWS.

OH?

THE GOOD NEWS IS DAD'S NOT GOING TO TRY TO FIGURE OUT THE TAXES HIMSELF THIS YEAR.

JASON, THAT'S NOT JUST GOOD NEWS.

THAT'S **GREAT** NEWS. **INCREDIBLE** NEWS. THE SORT OF NEWS I'VE PRAYED TO HEAR EVERY APRIL FOR THE LAST 19 YEARS.

WHAT'S THE BAD NEWS?

HE'S DOING THEM ON THE COMPUTER.

LIKEWISE, THAT'S NOT JUST BAD NEWS...

ARE FLOPPY DISKS SUPPOSED TO SNAP IN HALF LIKE THIS?

I DON'T GET IT — THE STUPID PROGRAM WON'T INSTALL!

DAD, **DUH!** YOU BOUGHT THE WINDOWS VERSION!

SO?

SO WE DON'T **HAVE** WINDOWS!

THE TAXINATOR

ARE YOU NUTS?! THERE'S A WINDOW RIGHT THERE!

WOULD YOU **LIKE** ME TO GO NUTS?

HOW ARE THE TAXES COMING ALONG?

ANDY, PLEASE!

IT'S HARD ENOUGH TO DO THIS **WITHOUT** YOU LOOKING OVER MY SHOULDER EVERY TWO SECONDS!

JUST REMEMBER THEY'RE DUE ON MONDAY.

LOOK, I KNOW WHAT I'M DOING, OK?!

...SAID GENERAL CUSTER TO HIS TROOPS.

HA-HA.

:Beep: Hard disk not found.

ANDY, THIS TAX SOFTWARE IS GREAT.

I JUST PUNCH IN THE NUMBERS FROM OUR W-2 FORMS AND VOILÀ, IT SAYS WE HAVE A REFUND COMING OF $37,400,591.

NOT THAT YOU DON'T STILL NEED TO DOUBLE-CHECK ALL THE FIGURES.

REMIND ME TO BE OUT OF TOWN WHEN THE AUDIT TEAM ARRIVES.

AAAA! WHAT HAPPENED TO MY TAX RETURNS?!

OH, IS **THAT** WHAT THAT BIG FILE WAS?

THE HARD DISK WAS FULL, SO I DELETED IT TO MAKE ROOM FOR MY NEW MARS COLONY SIMULATOR.

YOU **DO** HAVE A BACKUP COPY SOMEWHERE, RIGHT?

DAD, DON'T THINK OF THIS AS YOUR WORST NIGHTMARE COME TRUE... THINK OF IT AS A VALUABLE LIFE LESSON.

SON, IF IT WEREN'T FOR THE FACT THAT I NEED YOU AS A DEPENDENT.

I THINK I'VE FIGURED OUT WHY THE IRS MAKES THESE TAX FORMS SO COMPLICATED.

OH?

AFTER THE HOURS SPENT WADING THROUGH THE INSTRUCTIONS, AFTER DOING ALL THE MATH, AFTER **RE**-DOING ALL THE MATH, AFTER FINALLY FIGURING OUT WHAT WE OWE...

...IT'S ALMOST A RELIEF TO PUT THE CHECK IN THE MAIL.

EMPHASIS ON "ALMOST."

DO WE EVEN **HAVE** THIS MUCH MONEY?

FoxTrot
BILL AMEND

FOX!... YES, COACH?

I KNOW I USUALLY KEEP YOU ON THE BENCH. I KNOW ORDINARILY I'D MAKE YOU SIT HERE IN THE DUGOUT FOR THE WHOLE GAME.

BUT TODAY, FOX, I REALLY NEED YOUR HUSTLE. REALLY??

HERE'S A BUCK. RUN DOWN TO THE STORE AND GET ME SOME MORE SUNFLOWER SEEDS. YOU GOT IT, COACH!

HERE ARE THE SUNFLOWER SEEDS YOU WANTED, COACH. FOX, I'VE GOT BAD NEWS.

PRITCHARD'S BEEN EJECTED. I NEED YOU TO FILL IN AT SECOND WHEN WE TAKE THE FIELD.

I'M GOING TO PLAY SECOND BASE?! I'M GOING TO PLAY SECOND BASE?! RIGHT. NOW QUIT YAPPING AND GET READY.

BAD NEWS FOR THE OTHER TEAM IS RIGHT. THIS DUGOUT NEEDS BEER.

FOX, I WANT YOU TO GO OUT THERE AND MAKE A DIFFERENCE. WILL DO, COACH!

WHAP!

PETER, WHAT ARE YOU DOING?! THROW IT TO FIRST!

I MEANT IN A **GOOD** WAY, FOX. HEH HEH. SORRY. — DON'T THROW — IT **NOW**!

IF HE BUNTS, COVER FIRST...

IF HE BUNTS, COVER FIRST...

IF HE —...

ZING!

IN RETROSPECT, IT PROBABLY MAKES MORE SENSE TO PLAN FOR LINE DRIVES.

NICE CATCH.

I'VE REALLY GOT TO START TIMING MY SLIDES A LITTLE BETTER.

FOUL BALL, FOX. GO BACK TO FIRST.

WHERE'S PETER?

HE WENT UPSTAIRS TO TAKE A SHOWER.

HOW WAS HIS BASE-BALL GAME?

LET'S PUT IT THIS WAY: THE ENTIRE TEAM MOBBED PETER, HOISTED HIM ONTO THEIR SHOULDERS AND CARRIED HIM OFF THE FIELD.

... AFTER THREE INNINGS.

OUCH. POOR KID.

THE BEST GAME I'VE BEEN TO ALL YEAR.

FoxTrot
BILL AMEND

COWS CHEW THEIR CUD...

DOGS CHEW BONES...

KIDS CHEW GUM.

NOT IN **MY** CLASS, THEY DON'T.

IS THERE A SINGLE PRIMAL INSTINCT THAT **IS** ALLOWED IN SCHOOL?!

ROGER, I DON'T THINK I REMEMBER THE LAST TIME YOU AND I WENT OUT.

SURE YOU DO.

LAST WEEKEND. WE TOOK THOSE BOTTLES DOWN TO THE RECYCLING CENTER.

ROGER, I DON'T THINK YOU REMEMBER WHAT IT **MEANS** TO GO OUT.

WHAT ABOUT THE TRIP WE TOOK TO SEARS?

PETER, DON'T FORGET TO TAKE OUT THE TRASH.

NAG, NAG, NAG.

I HEARD THAT.

HEARD WHAT?

YOU JUST CALLED ME A NAG! I HEARD IT PLAIN AS DAY!

I DIDN'T! I SWEAR!

JASON, LET ME SEE THAT BOOK YOU'VE BEEN READING.

UM, WHY?

BLUE JELLO IS BY FAR MY FAVORITE.

WITH RED JELLO, YOU GET TO PRETEND IT'S GELATINIZED BRAIN JUICE, BUT WITH **BLUE** JELLO, IT'S MORE LIKE GELATINIZED SPACE ALIEN BRAIN JUICE.

WANNA KNOW WHAT I PRETEND THE BANANA SLICES ARE?

WHY IS IT YOU ALWAYS SEEM TO END UP WITH **TWO** BOWLS OF THAT STUFF?

C'MON, FOX!

LIFT IT! LIFT IT!

MORE! MORE! MORE!

NEVER SAY OUT LOUD THAT GYM IS YOUR EASIEST CLASS.

BETCHER VEINS DON'T DO THAT IN PHYSICS, NOW DO THEY BOY?

PAIGE, I'VE FIGURED OUT WHY YOU'RE SO AFRAID OF QUINCY.

AND WHY'S THAT?

THE TWO OF YOU NEVER HAD A CHANCE TO BOND PROPERLY.

AAAA!

I'LL BET BY THIS TIME TOMORROW, YOU'LL BE INSEPARABLE.

JASON, IF THIS WET STUFF ON HIS CHEST IS GLUE...

FoxTrot
BILL AMEND

MOTHERRR!

PAIGE, WHAT'S WRONG?

SLAM!

THESE WEIRDOS KEEP CALLING ME UP! I DON'T EVEN KNOW WHO THEY ARE! THIS ONE GUY CALLED FROM NORWAY!

WHAT THE HECK IS GOING ON?!

WELL, IF I HAD TO GUESS...

THE INTERNET: THE ULTIMATE BATHROOM WALL.

HOW'S THIS? "FOR A REALLY REALLY GOOD TIME, CALL PAIGE AT-..."

MOM, PAIGE PUNCHED ME IN THE STOMACH AND NOW I'M COUGHING UP BLOOD.

COUGH COUGH

SEE?? I THINK YOU SHOULD TAKE AWAY HER ALLOWANCE AND GIVE IT TO ME.

JASON, THAT'S KETCHUP.

YOU KNOW, IT'S POSSIBLE MY BLOOD IS JUST NATURALLY THICK AND ZESTY.

SON, JUST HOW MANY COLAS DID YOU AND MARCUS DRINK TODAY?

DR. TING, HAVE I EVER TOLD YOU WHAT A WONDERFUL TEACHER I THINK YOU ARE?

I MEAN, YOU'RE SO NICE... SO FRIENDLY... SO WITH-IT...

SO SMART...

NO, PAIGE, YOU CAN'T HAVE AN EXTENSION ON YOUR LAB REPORT.

MAYBE TOO SMART.

THANKS, BY THE WAY, FOR THE CHOCOLATES.

FoxTrot
BILL AMEND

HERE COMES JACK PRAHL. CHECK THE LIST.

LET'S SEE...

AS OF 9:00 A.M. THIS MORNING, JACK PRAHL HAD NO PROM DATE.

♪ YOOO HOOO... JACKIE-POOOO...

PUT A STAR NEXT TO HIS NAME — HE LOOKED OUR WAY.

WITH EXTRA-BIG EYES.

THE PROM IS A WEEK AND A HALF AWAY AND NO ONE'S EVEN COME **CLOSE** TO ASKING ME!

PAIGE, DON'T FEEL BAD.

YOU'RE A FRESHMAN! **NOBODY** INVITES A FRESHMAN! FRESHMEN ARE DIRT! BACTERIA! HUMAN POND SCUM!

I MEAN, IF SOMEONE ACTUALLY **DID** ASK YOU, I'D BE AFRAID THEY WERE DERANGED OR SOMETHING.

PETER, AS MUCH AS I APPRECIATE YOUR ATTEMPTS TO CHEER ME UP...

HECK, **I** ONLY TALK TO YOU BECAUSE YOU'RE MY SISTER.

YOU KNOW, PAIGE, MAYBE WE'RE GOING ABOUT THIS ALL WRONG.

MAYBE INSTEAD OF LETTING GUYS KNOW HOW DESPERATE WE ARE TO GO TO THE PROM, WE SHOULD BE PLAYING HARD TO GET.

IT'S WORTH A TRY.

HI. I WAS, UM, WONDERING IF EITHER OF YOU WOULD CONSIDER...

IS HE TALKING TO US?

HO-HUM. I SUPPOSE SO.

(GULP) NEVER MIND.

WAIT!

The Tribune

GIRL, 14, NOT ASKED TO PROM

"Paige _who_?," says one boy

The Register

GIRL, 14 TO WATCH TV AT HOME WHILE REST OF SCHOOL PARTIES

Prom will be "best ever," say organizers

The Times

GIRL, 14, NAMED "MOST PATHETIC" IN NATIONWIDE POLL

"Unanimous vote," says Gallup source

I'VE GOT TO STOP NODDING OFF IN JOURNALISM CLASS.

THIS IS RIDICULOUS, NICOLE! IT'S LIKE WE'RE THE ONLY GIRLS IN SCHOOL THAT HAVEN'T BEEN ASKED TO THE PROM!

PAIGE, THAT'S NOT TRUE.

WELL, I KNOW I'M EXAGGERATING A LITTLE, BUT...

I MEAN THE, UM, "WE" PART.

I DIDN'T KNOW HOW TO TELL YOU. BENNY WHITE ASKED ME THIS MORNING.

EXCUSE ME WHILE I PRAY FOR THE EARTH TO SWALLOW ME UP.

THE WEIRD THING IS I THOUGHT FOR SURE HE LIKED YOU BETTER.

NICOLE, I CAN'T BELIEVE YOU SAID "YES"! I CAN'T BELIEVE YOU'RE ACTUALLY GOING TO THE PROM!

THERE YOU'LL BE, HAVING THE TIME OF YOUR LIFE WITH SOME BOY, WHILE I, YOUR BEST FRIEND SINCE FOURTH GRADE, SIT ALONE AT HOME, CRYING MY EYES OUT.

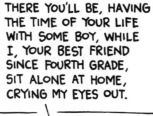

HOW CAN YOU DO THIS TO ME?!

FoxTrot
BILL AMEND

PAIGE, WHAT DO YOU WANT ME TO DO?!

STAY HOME FROM THE PROM JUST BECAUSE YOU'RE NOT GOING?!

I CAN'T DO THAT! I'VE DREAMED OF GOING TO A PROM SINCE I WAS A LITTLE GIRL! I'VE LIVED FOR THIS OPPORTUNITY FOR AS LONG AS I CAN REMEMBER!

LOOK, IT'LL PROBABLY BE REALLY BORING.

WHERE'S A TELEPORTATION DEVICE WHEN YOU NEED ONE?

SLAM!

PAIGE, I WISH YOU'D CALM DOWN.

CALM DOWN?! AFTER WHAT NICOLE'S DONE TO ME?!

MOTHER, SUPPOSE **YOUR** BEST FRIEND WAS GOING TO SATURDAY'S PROM WITH SOME CUTE BOY WHILE YOU WERE LEFT TO TWIDDLE YOUR THUMBS AT HOME — HOW WOULD **YOU** REACT?!

WELL, CONSIDERING THAT MY BEST FRIEND IS 45, MALE AND MARRIED...

I SWEAR, I HAVE A GOOD MIND TO STEW RIGHT THROUGH "MELROSE".

PAIGE, SWEETIE, WHY CAN'T YOU JUST BE **HAPPY** FOR NICOLE?

WHAT??

YOU KNOW HOW MUCH THE PROM MEANS TO HER. YOU SHOULD BE HAPPY SHE'S GETTING TO GO, EVEN IF YOU AREN'T. SHE'S YOUR BEST FRIEND.

HAPPY FOR **HER**?! SHE'S DESERTING ME, MOTHER! SHE'S LEAVING ME MISERABLE AND ALONE! SHE SHOULD BE STAYING HOME WITH **ME**!

TALK ABOUT SELFISH...

MY POINT EXACTLY!

YOU SHOULD KNOW THAT I'M NOT TALKING TO YOU ANYMORE.

WELL, I'M NOT TALKING TO **YOU** ANYMORE.

FINE.

FINE.

HEY, GUYS— WAIT UP!

WELL, MAYBE I'LL TALK TO YOU A **LITTLE**...

MY GOD, DID YOU SEE HER SKIRT?!

NICOLE, I'M SORRY I'VE BEEN SO PETTY ABOUT THINGS.

IT'S JUST THAT I REALLY, REALLY, REALLY, **REALLY** WANTED TO GO TO THE PROM AND I'M NOT, AND WHEN I FOUND OUT YOU **WERE**, WELL, IT KINDA HIT A NERVE. WILL YOU FORGIVE ME?

YEAH.

REALLY? JUST LIKE THAT?

REALLY.

SEE, NOW **I'D** HAVE MADE ME GROVEL.

WOULDN'T THAT BE A LITTLE, OH, WHAT'S THE WORD?

IS IT OK IF I GO TO THE MALL WITH NICOLE?

I TAKE IT THE TWO OF YOU HAVE PATCHED UP YOUR DIFFERENCES.

MOSTLY, YEAH. WE AGREED THAT SHE SHOULD GO TO THE PROM AND HAVE A GOOD TIME AND I SHOULD STOP WALLOWING IN SELF-PITY. LIFE'S TOO SHORT AND OUR FRIENDSHIP'S TOO IMPORTANT.

BUT THERE IS STILL A LARGER ISSUE TO RESOLVE THAT I FEAR MAY REALLY TEAR US APART.

WHICH IS?

DRESS COLOR. SHE WANTS THIS TOTALLY GROSS BLUE THING.

WELL, PAIGE, GOOD FRIEND-SHIPS DO TAKE WORK.

FoxTrot
BILL AMEND

WELL, HERE WE ARE... THE LAIR OF THE SLIME DEMON.

SOMEHOW I IMAGINED IT BEING MORE LIKE MY SISTER'S ROOM.

THIS DOES SEEM LESS DEADLY.

LET ME GO FIRST AND USE MY FIREBALL SPELL.

WATCH OUT—THESE ELVES HAVE +2 CROSSBOWS.

I DON'T BELIEVE THIS.

WHAT?

WHAT?

IT'S A BEAUTIFUL SPRING DAY AND YOU TWO BOYS ARE SITTING HERE IN FRONT OF THE TV, PLAYING THAT SILLY "DUNGEONSTALKER" VIDEO GAME!

CALL ME OLD-FASHIONED, BUT WHEN I WAS YOUR AGE, BOYS LIKED TO PLAY **REAL** GAMES. GAMES LIKE BASEBALL OR SOCCER OR BASKETBALL!...

I SUPPOSE A LITTLE BASEBALL MIGHT BE FUN.

I'D PLAY.

GOOD. LET ME GO TELL YOUR FATHER, JASON. I'LL BET HE'D LIKE TO PLAY, TOO.

OUCH. I CAN'T BELIEVE MY RIGHT FIELDER DROPPED THAT.

HERE COMES YOUR DAD. WHY'S HE WEARING THAT WEIRD GLOVE?

AMEND

Marry hat hey lid tell lam, ids fleas woes wide has know.

INITIATING SPELL CHECK...

BEEP. NO ERRORS FOUND.

IF YOU EVER WANT TO FEEL SUPERIOR TO A COMPUTER...

PETER, I SPECIFICALLY ASKED YOU TO NOT FINISH THE MILK!

AND I DIDN'T! HONEST! I SWEAR!

SEE? THERE'S AT LEAST FIVE OR SIX DROPS LEFT.

YOU KNOW, IT'S KIDS LIKE YOU THAT GROW UP TO BE LAWYERS.

If Farmer Bob's field is a circle of radius 300 meters, and $A = \pi r^2$...

JASON, WHAT'S PI?

3.14...

...159265358979323 8462643383279502 8841971693993751 0582097494459230 781640628620899...

MOTHER, HOW IS THIS **MY** FAULT?!

...712268 0661300 1927876 6111959 09...

FoxTrot
BILL AMEND

AAAA! WE'RE OUT OF ALPHA-BITS!

SO?

SO I HAVE MY ENGLISH FINAL TODAY! I **ALWAYS** EAT ALPHA-BITS BEFORE AN ENGLISH TEST! THEY FUEL MY VERBAL SKILLS! WITHOUT THEM I'M DEAD!

THERE'S GOT TO BE SOMETHING I CAN DO...

LUCKY CHARMS! DO WE HAVE ANY LUCKY CHARMS?!

WOULDN'T SOMETHING **FLAKY** BE A LITTLE MORE UP YOUR ALLEY?

STUDENTS, BEFORE I PASS OUT YOUR EXAMS, I SHOULD REMIND YOU THAT THIS TEST WILL CONSTITUTE A QUARTER OF YOUR FINAL GRADE, SO GOOD LUCK.

HERE YOU GO, MR. FOX...

HEE HEE... HEE HEE HEE... WAAA HA HA HA HA HA HA HA HA HA...

I'M SORRY. I WAS JUST STRUCK BY THE IRONY OF THE LETTER "A" ON YOUR CAP.

UM, SIR? THE CLIFFS NOTES DIDN'T MENTION THIS CHARACTER.

WELL, STEVE, IT TOOK AN ALL-NIGHTER, BUT I DID IT.

I MEMORIZED EVERY PAGE OF THIS PHYSICS TEXTBOOK. EVERY FORMULA... EVERY LAW... EVERY THEORY... COLD. TODAY'S TEST WILL BE A WALK IN THE PARK.

SERIOUSLY, I MEMORIZED EVERYTHING.

EXCEPT MAYBE THE EXAM SCHEDULE.

AAA! TODAY'S THE **HISTORY** FINAL ?!?...

PHYSICS IS ON FRIDAY.

DON'T START THE TEST UNTIL I'VE PASSED THEM ALL OUT.

I WILL NOT BE PSYCHED OUT BY MY MATH **TEACHER**, EITHER.

HEE HEE HEE...

MISS O'MALLEY? I THINK THIS TEST HAS A MISTAKE IN IT.

OH?

QUESTION 2(a) ASKS FOR THE DECIMAL EQUIVALENT OF 1/10. THIS IS WAY TOO EASY.

SURELY YOU MEANT TO ASK FOR THE DECIMAL EQUIVALENT OF SOMETHING CHALLENGING LIKE $1/\sqrt{2}$.

I STILL DON'T UNDERSTAND WHY SHE WOULD SEND YOU HOME EARLY.

WELL, IT WAS RIGHT ABOUT THEN THAT THE PENCILS STARTED FLYING.

IT'S SUMMER VACATION!

94 DAYS WITHOUT A SINGLE HOMEWORK ASSIGNMENT OR TEST!

94 DAYS! THAT'S 2,256 HOURS! 135,360 MINUTES! 8,121,600 SECONDS!

OF COURSE, MY MATH BRAIN WAITS UNTIL **NOW** TO SHOW UP.

FoxTrot
BILL AMEND

LAZY DAYS OF SUMMER...

...MEET THE LAZY BOYS OF SUMMER.

HI THERE.

SO, PETE, WHAT DO YOU HAVE PLANNED FOR THE SUMMER?

WELL, MY DAD KNOWS THIS ONE GUY WHO NEEDS A STOCKBOY FOR HIS HARDWARE STORE...

HE KNOWS ANOTHER GUY WHO NEEDS SOMEONE TO HELP PAINT HOUSES...

HIS SECRETARY'S HUSBAND'S COMPANY IS HIRING TEEN-AGERS FOR THEIR MAILROOM...

AND HE CALLED HOME AT LUNCH TO SAY HE HAD A HALF-DOZEN OTHER JOB LEADS TO TELL ME ABOUT.

SO, BASICALLY, YOU'LL SPEND THE SUMMER HIDING FROM YOUR DAD.

I JUST WISH MY NOT WORKING DIDN'T REQUIRE SO MUCH WORK.

YOU KNOW, MARCUS, IF WE GET REALLY GOOD AT THIS, MAYBE WE CAN MAKE THE '96 OLYMPIC TEAM.

TWANG!

TWANG!

WOULD THAT BE IN ARCHERY OR SPRINTING?

OF COURSE, WE'D ALSO HAVE TO BE **ALIVE** IN '96...

I SHOT AN ARROW INTO THE AIR...

...IT FELL TO EARTH, IN PAIGE'S HAIR.

ARE YOU FAMILIAR WITH THE PHRASE "BEAT POET"?!

I SHOT ANOTHER ARROW INTO THE AIR..

I THINK I MAY HAVE TO FIND A NEW SPORT TO PURSUE.

OH?

ARCHERY IS FUN, BUT IT'S JUST TOO DARN EXPENSIVE.

THE EQUIPMENT COSTS THAT MUCH?

WHEN YOU HAVE TO BUY IT OVER AND OVER AND OVER AGAIN.

AH...

KISS THAT BOW GOODBYE, PAL.

FoxTrot
BILL AMEND

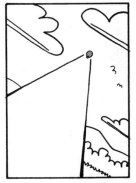

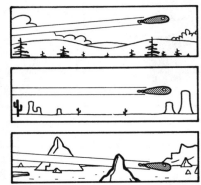

THE BEST THING ABOUT BUBBLE GUM ART IS YOU DON'T NEED NAILS TO HANG IT.

CAN I HELP YOU?

YES. DO YOU HAVE THE SUNGLASSES THAT FOX MULDER WEARS ON "THE X-FILES"?

THAT WOULD BE THESE. I TAKE IT YOU'RE A BIG FAN OF THE SHOW.

NOT PARTICULARLY.

THEN WHY, IF YOU DON'T MIND MY ASKING...

OH, JASONNN...

AAAA! I WANTED TO GET THOSE!

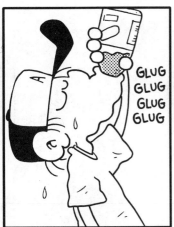

GLUG GLUG GLUG GLUG

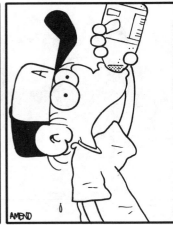

MOM, I REALLY WISH YOU WOULDN'T STORE LEFTOVER CHICKEN BROTH IN OLD SNAPPLE BOTTLES.

I DON'T.

YOU KNOW, I THINK I WILL GO PLAY OUTSIDE...

FoxTrot
BILL AMEND

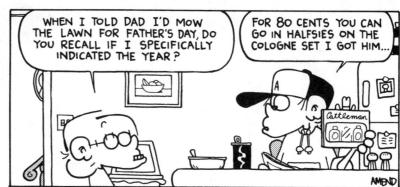

WHEN I TOLD DAD I'D MOW THE LAWN FOR FATHER'S DAY, DO YOU RECALL IF I SPECIFICALLY INDICATED THE YEAR?

FOR 80 CENTS YOU CAN GO IN HALFSIES ON THE COLOGNE SET I GOT HIM...